A Note to Parents and Caregivers:

Read-it! Joke Books are for children who are moving ahead on the amazing road to reading. These fun books support the acquisition and extension of reading skills as well as a love of books.

Published by the same company that produces *Read-it!* Readers, these books introduce the question/answer and dialogue patterns that help children expand their thinking about language structure and book formats.

When sharing joke books with a child, read in short stretches. Pause often to talk about the meaning of the jokes. The question/answer and dialogue formats work well for this purpose and provide an opportunity to talk about the language and meaning of the jokes. Have the child turn the pages and point to the pictures and familiar words. When you read the jokes, have fun creating the voices of characters or emphasizing some important words. Be sure to reread favorite jokes.

There is no right or wrong way to share books with children. Find time to read with your child, and pass on the legacy of literacy.

Adria F. Klein, Ph.D.
Professor Emeritus
California State University
San Bernardino, California

Managing Editors: Bob Temple, Catherine Neitge
Creative Director: Terri Foley
Editors: Jerry Ruff, Christianne Jones
Designer: Les Tranby
Page production: Picture Window Books
The illustrations in this book were rendered digitally.

Picture Window Books
5115 Excelsior Boulevard
Suite 232
Minneapolis, MN 55416
877-845-8392
www.picturewindowbooks.com

Printed in the United States of America.

Library of Congress Cataloging-in-Publication Data
Moore, Mark, 1947-
Beastly laughs : a book of monster jokes / by Mark Moore ;
illustrated by Anne Haberstroh.
p. cm. — (Read-it! joke books—supercharged!)
ISBN 1-4048-0625-3
1. Monsters—Juvenile humor. 2. Wit and humor, Juvenile.
I. Title. II. Series.

PN6231.M665M66 2004
818'.602—dc22   2004007317

Beastly Laughs

A Book of Monster Jokes

By Mark Moore • Illustrated by Anne Haberstroh

Reading Advisers:
Adria F. Klein, Ph.D.
Professor Emeritus, California State University
San Bernardino, California

Susan Kesselring, M.A., Literacy Educator
Rosemount-Apple Valley-Eagan (Minnesota) School District

PICTURE WINDOW BOOKS
Minneapolis, Minnesota

What do you call zombies
with lots of kids?

Mom-sters.

What is a monster's favorite
part of a joke?

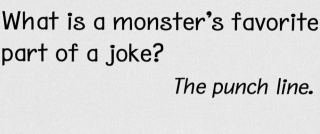

> The punch line.

Why did the invisible man
look in the mirror?

> To see if he wasn't there.

What happened when Dracula
met the werewolf?

> They fought tooth and nail.

What is Bigfoot's favorite cheese?

> Monster-ella.

Why wasn't Dr. Frankenstein ever lonely?

Because he was so good at making new friends.

What did the director say when he finished his mummy movie?

"That's a wrap."

Which side of a monster's mouth has the sharpest teeth?

The inside.

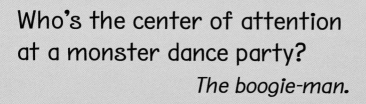

Who's the center of attention
at a monster dance party?

The boogie-man.

Why did King Kong climb to the top
of the Empire State Building?

He was too big to use the elevator.

How did the giant snake find out
that he wasn't poisonous?

He bit his tongue—and lived.

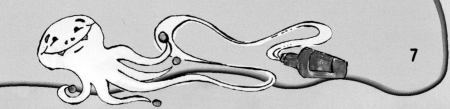

7

What is a monster's favorite
sweet treat?

> *Ghoul Scout cookies.*

What do sea monsters eat?

> *Fish and ships.*

What do you call a monster who
tells long, terrible stories?

> *A giant boar.*

Why was the monster lonely
on Halloween?

> *Because he missed
> his mummy.*

When a monster puts his
tooth under his pillow,
who comes to get it?

The tooth scary.

What do you call Bigfoot in
a telephone booth?

Stuck.

What would you get if you crossed
Godzilla with a teacher?

*You'd get the kids to
pay attention in class.*

How do you contact an
undersea monster?

You drop it a line.

Why didn't the giant snake
use silverware?

> *Because he had
> a forked tongue.*

How do you keep Godzilla
from smelling?

> *Plug his nose.*

Why was the monster pulling
the rope?

> *Have you ever tried
> to push one?*

What does Dr. Frankenstein's monster like for breakfast?

A big jolt of juice.

What time is it when a monster comes for dinner?

Time to leave.

What monster wears a mask and has a long, gray trunk?

The Ele-phantom of the Opera.

Why are some monsters so quiet?

Because silence is ghoul-den.

How do you make a green monster?

Cross a blue one with a yellow one.

What's the Abominable Snowman's favorite game?

Freeze tag.

When do monsters eat breakfast?

Never before moaning.

What did the dragon say when he found the knight hiding under a rock?

"You're toast."

Why did the monster eat
the street lamp?
> *Because he wanted*
> *a light snack.*

Why didn't the monster eat
the comedian?
> *Because he tasted funny.*

What happened when the monster
ran away with the circus?
> *The police made him*
> *bring it back.*

Why did the mummy need
a vacation?

He was coming unraveled.

What do you get Godzilla
for his birthday?

Whatever he wants.

What has sharp claws and fangs
and is green and slimy?

*I don't know, but it's
crawling on your neck!*

What position does a monster
play in soccer?

Ghoul-ie.

What's Godzilla's favorite sport?

Dragon racing.

Monster:
 "I've been seeing spots."
Dr. Frankenstein:
 "Have you seen a doctor?"
Monster:
 "No, just spots."

Why did the monster eat people's brains?
 He wanted food for thought.

What should you do if you find a monster in your bed?
 Sleep in the guest room.

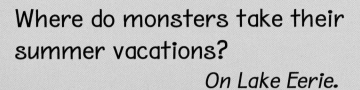

Where do monsters take their summer vacations?

> *On Lake Eerie.*

Where do monsters go to college?

> *At goon-iversities.*

Why do zombies make such good gardeners?

> *Because they have green thumbs.*

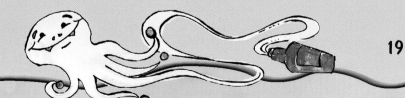

19

Why was the Abominable
Snowman so popular?

Because he was cool.

What movie do monsters
watch again and again?
> Scar Wars.

What do you say to a
three-headed monster?
> *"Hello! Hello! Hello!"*

Why do monsters make
such good hosts?
> *Because they like to have
> their friends for lunch.*

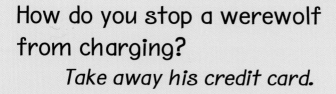

How do you stop a werewolf
from charging?
> *Take away his credit card.*

What did the space monster
say to the textbook?

"Take me to your reader."

What's the best way to get
King Kong moving?

A crane and a semitruck.

Why did the monster throw
the dog a baseball?

*Because he liked to
play with his food.*

What are giant alligator
skins used for?

*To hold giant
alligators together.*

What's the one-eyed monster's
favorite reference book?

The en-cyclops-edia.

Why is the monster's bark
worse than his bite?

He has bad breath.

Look for all of the books in this series:

Read-it! Joke Books—Supercharged!

Beastly Laughs
A Book of Monster Jokes

Chalkboard Chuckles
A Book of Classroom Jokes

Creepy Crawlers
A Book of Bug Jokes

Roaring with Laughter
A Book of Animal Jokes

Sit! Stay! Laugh!
A Book of Pet Jokes

Spooky Sillies
A Book of Ghost Jokes

Read-it! Joke Books

Alphabet Soup
A Book of Riddles About Letters

Animal Quack-Ups
Foolish and Funny Jokes About Animals

Bell Buzzers
A Book of Knock-Knock Jokes

Chewy Chuckles
Deliciously Funny Jokes About Food

Crazy Criss-Cross
A Book of Mixed-Up Riddles

Ding Dong
A Book of Knock-Knock Jokes

Dino Rib Ticklers
Hugely Funny Jokes About Dinosaurs

Doctor, Doctor
A Book of Doctor Jokes

Door Knockers
A Book of Knock-Knock Jokes

Family Funnies
A Book of Family Jokes

Funny Talk
A Book of Silly Riddles

Galactic Giggles
Far-Out and Funny Jokes About Outer Space

Laughs on a Leash
A Book of Pet Jokes

Monster Laughs
Frightfully Funny Jokes About Monsters

Nutty Neighbors
A Book of Knock-Knock Jokes

Open Up and Laugh!
A Book of Knock-Knock Jokes

Rhyme Time
A Book of Rhyming Riddles

School Buzz
Classy and Funny Jokes About School

School Daze
A Book of Riddles About School

Teacher Says
A Book of Teacher Jokes

Three-Alarm Jokes
A Book of Firefighter Jokes

Under Arrest
A Book of Police Jokes

Who's There?
A Book of Knock-Knock Jokes

Zoodles
A Book of Riddles About Animals

24